The
INFANT JESUS
OF PRAGUE

National Shrine of the Infant Jesus of Prague
Prague, Okla.

The
INFANT JESUS
OF PRAGUE

By
REV. LUDVIK NEMEC

**Prayers to the Infant Jesus for All Occasions
with
A Short History of the Devotion**

Illustrated

CATHOLIC BOOK PUBLISHING CO.
NEW YORK

NIHIL OBSTAT: Daniel V. Flynn, J.C.D.
Censor Librorum
IMPRIMATUR: Joseph T. O'Keefe
Vicar General, Archdiocese of New York

(T-129)

5 6 7 8 9 10 11 12 13 14 15

PREFACE

THIS new book in honor of the Infant Jesus of Prague is the result of an extensive research into all available historical as well as ecclesiastical sources relating to the devotion to the Infant. Documents of the Sacred Roman Congregations as well as privileges granted by various Popes were consulted to establish clear official approval of the devotion.

Abundant material in various modern languages—Czech, English, French, German, Italian, Polish, Portuguese, Slovak, Spanish, etc.—was especially helpful in an effort to show the prayerful mind that it must first understand devotionally the historical promise of the Infant of Prague ("The more you honor Me, the more I will bless you!") before it can fully reap its rich benefits.

I am indebted to many authors and publishers of foreign language works which provided helpful guidelines, to many Sisters' convents and monasteries who gave information of their novenas, and to hundreds of devotional booklets, novena leaflets, and prayerbooks for the reconstruction of devotional practices of all kinds. All historical prayers were taken from P. Emmerich of St. Stephen, *Pragerisches Gross und Klein* (Prague, 1737) as rendered into English in my book *The Great and Little One of Prague* (1959).

It is my fervent hope that this little book will win fresh love for the Divine Infant and direct the steps of countless Catholics to the veneration of the Infant Jesus.

CONTENTS

The Statue of the Holy Child of Prague
in its shrine in Prague.

Part I
History of the Holy Child of Prague

Origin in Spain

THE origin of the miraculous statue is Spanish. In 1556 Maria Manriquez de Lara brought this precious family heirloom with her to Bohemia, a part of the present Czechoslovakia, when she married the Czech nobleman, Vratislav of Pernstyn.

Spain at that time excelled in spiritual strength, especially with the mysticism of the great St. Teresa of Avila (1582). She emphasized the devotion of the Holy Childhood, and the humane littleness of God's greatness as a means of establishing the proper relationship of creatures to their Creator. Her mysticism found a way to express these spiritual values in the representation of the Holy Child as King, Whom only the little ones are willing and able to worship. The best reflection of this is embodied in the miraculous statue of the Infant of Prague.

However, the home of the Infant is the city of Prague, capital of Czechoslovakia, a city in which every stone speaks of rich history. It is housed in the church of Our Lady of Victory from which it provides spiritual uplift for millions who have adopted the Holy Infant's call to humility, simplicity, and sincerity—to become little in order to become great and pleasing before Christ the King.

9

This mystery, this effective spiritual meditation, is the reason why the Infant of Prague is so continuously appealing to human hearts over all the world, which He has so firmly in His hands. One can find His statue in almost every church, convent, monastery and house, representing a Divine Protection toward His devotees.

Image of the Infant

VESTED and adorned, the image of the Infant of Prague is quite different from the Child depicted in centuries of Christian art as the Babe of Bethlehem, wrapped in swaddling clothes, in the manger of the nativity scene. More like the Child visited by the Magi than the Infant adored by the Christmas shepherds, the miraculous image of the Infant of Prague, eighteen inches high, stands on a broad pedestal and is firmly embedded to the waist in a silver case.

The slender and beautifully-modeled figure is carved of wood thinly coated with wax, with the left foot barely visible under a long white tunic. The left hand encircles a miniature globe, surmounted by a cross, signifying the world-wide kingship of the Christ Child. The right hand is extended in blessing, in a form reserved for the Supreme Pontiff; that is, the first two fingers are upraised to symbolize the two natures in Christ, while the folded thumb and last two fingers touch each other, representing the unity of the Father, the Son, and the Holy Spirit in the mystery of the Blessed Trinity.

Adorning the fingers of the statue since May, 1788, are two jeweled rings, gifts of the nobleman De la Haye and his wife, in grateful remembrance of a miraculous cure worked in favor of their dying daughter. The head of the image is covered with a wig of human blond hair, a substitute for the former white wig indicated in old carvings and pictures. Affixed to the case, but apparently resting on the head, is the crown which was presented by Bernard Ignatius Martinic, supreme burgrave of the Czech kingdom. This crown was blessed in a solemn coronation ceremony.

The face of the image does not have the regular classical features typical of many later statues, but it has a strange power of evoking sentiments of deep gratitude for the mystery of God-made-Man. Yet for all His majestic posture and regal attire the little King of Prague is more striking for His outward expression of human littleness than by the impression of hidden greatness.

Wardrobe of the Infant

THE wardrobe of the Infant of Prague resembles liturgical vestments. The inner garments are similar to the priest's alb; one is of white linen, simply made; the other is of lace. Covering these is a dalmatic made of silk, velvet, or damask, over which is worn a cape, a miniature liturgical cope. Still preserved are the original garments worn by the statue when it arrived in Bohemia, the gift of Princess Polyxena Lobkowitz.

The vestments are changed according to the liturgical season, a custom dating from 1713, the year in which thousands lost their lives in the cholera epidemic which raged in Prague. The Carmelites received expressions of gratitude from many of the pious faithful who had been spared. They gave permission to one of these, Anna Clare Loregin, to fashion new garments for the image and to change them periodically.

Some of the more exquisite garments dating from that time are made of heavy damask, richly woven with gold and embroidered with pearls. Of the thirty-nine sets, the most artistic and historically important are those presented by the Empress Maria Theresa, which are matched in richness only by the gold-embroidered red ones donated by Emperor Ferdinand.

Several sets of white, decorated with seed pearls and Czech garnents, and woven of blue and silver threads, were donated by persons now unknown. Among this collection is a rose-colored set interwoven with ribbon in rococo style.

Unique and unversally admired are the Chinese sets. One displays a motif that features oriental birds. Another, the gift of the Carmelites in Shanghai, is white, with chrysanthemum sprays embroidered along the hem to form Chinese characters which read: "Divine Infant Jesus, have mercy on China; return it to the faith and free it from the power of the evil spirit."

Along the sleeves is woven the prayer: "Jesus, Divine Child, Your kingdom come in China." An embroidered heart, set with coral and surrounded by a pearl-studded crown of thorns, adorns the front of the garment.

The English nuns from St. Joseph's Church in the Mala Strana quarter of Prague now enjoy the privilege of clothing the Infant; the change of vestments is usually made about ten o'clock in the morning after Mass. Various devotional objects, such as medals, pictures, and rosaries, are touched to the statue at this time, to be distributed to all parts of the world.

Princess Polyxena Lobkowitz inherited the statue from her mother and continued in the devotion at home. For the purpose of spreading this devotion publicly she presented this Image to the Discalced Carmelites in Prague in 1628.

First Apostle of the Devotion

FATHER Cyril of the Mother of God became the first zealous apostle and promoter of this devotion in gratitude for having been granted an assurance of his religious and priestly vocation. How the Infant King wished and even demanded to be venerated is a touching story, unique in that one can hardly find anything similar in the whole of hagiological literature.

It is truly a spiritual romance in which the human soul finds mystical joy in being subjected to its Master, the Infant King. All troubles seem to disappear with an unlimited confidence in the Powerful Infant, Who takes good care of all the needs of His subjects. This assurance springs from His historical promise: "The more you honor Me, the more I will bless you!"—the promise which became the cornerstone of this devotion.

This was the impulse that led the Carmelite Father Cyril to succeed in his efforts to bring the worship of the Infant to universal veneration. From the moment he heard personally from Polyxena those prophetic words: "I give you what I prize most highly in the world. As long as you venerate this Image, you shall not want!" until his death in 1675, he was zealous in spreading glory to the Little King.

He overcame all difficulties in the repair of the statue, lost and neglected in the trying time of the Thirty Years' War, and found in 1637, when he returned to Prague from Munich. When he found this statue in the debris, very dilapidated, he venerated it at first privately, and then publicly.

Statue Lost and Found

FOR seven years (1630-37) the statue of the Infant had lain in the dust, mutilated, unhonored and forgotten by all. This was the time when Father Cyril, then a novice, was sent with others from Prague to Munich, because the city of Prague was invaded by Swedish troops, and there was anti-Catholic vandalism. When, after the Treaty of

Prague in 1635, the situation became better the Carmelites returned to the monastery. But they had completely forgotten the statue in their anxiety for their daily bread.

The monks were so poor that they could not even pay the rent for their fields and vineyards. They were reduced to the sorest straits, and suffered bitter want. On Pentecost, in 1637, Father Cyril was sent back to Prague, and soon restored the veneration of the Infant of Prague.

Father Cyril had searched every corner of the cloister for the lost statue until at last he found the dusty image. Then he told his superior of all the graces the monastery enjoyed from the Infant in the past, and begged permission to place the statue in the oratory. Father Cyril was so overwhelmed with joy at finding the statue that he did not notice that the hands of the Infant were broken.

Confidence in the Statue

ONE day, long after the monks had left the oratory, he remained and knelt for hours before the statue, in mystic ecstasy, meditating on the Divine goodness. And something happened. He heard these words: "Have pity on Me and I will have pity on you. Give Me My hands and I will give you peace. The more you honor Me, the more I will bless you!" It was only then that Father Cyril saw the broken hands.

In his simplicity, Father Cyril was ashamed. Realizing that the Infant had broken hands, he hurried to the Prior, begging him to have the hands replaced. The Prior, not having the same deep understanding of the statue as Father Cyril, excused himself because of the great poverty of the monastery in not having the necessary means for the repair.

However Father Cyril did not give up. His complete confidence in the Infant was rewarded. A pious and wealthy man came to Prague and fell ill. It happened that Father Cyril was called to this dying man, who offered financial help to repair the Infant. The Prior bought a new statue instead of having the old one repaired. But this new statue was shattered by a falling candlestick the very first day.

This was an evident indication to Father Cyril that the wish of the Infant must be fulfilled literally. The Prior was not a hindrance for long. On account of continual unrest, sorrow, and trials of all sorts, he found himself compelled to retire from his office long before the expiration of his term.

Venerated by People and the Monks

THE sorrowing Father Cyril carried the statue to his cell and besought the Infant, through His Blessed Mother, to send the necessary money to the Prior. He had hardly finished his fervent prayers when he was called into the church. There he found a noble lady awaiting him, who greeted him and handed him a considerable amount of money. When he was about to thank her, the lady disappeared.

Full of joy, the happy Father Cyril thanked Our Lady of the Carmel, and took the money to the Prior, who consented to the mending of the statue provided that the expense would not exceed a certain sum. Unfortunately, it did exceed the sum in question, and again Father Cyril was denied his desire. But still he did not give up.

Thinking of how he could get the necessary money, he heard within his soul a voice saying: "Place Me at the entrance of the sacristy and you will receive aid!" He did so, and soon a stranger came into the sacristy and, noticing the broken hands of the statue of the Infant, offered to have them repaired. At the same moment, the Prior came in, and he gladly accepted the offer.

When the statue was repaired, it was placed in the church and exposed for a time for public veneration. But the monks still did not accept the veneration of the Infant as their primary object of importance. They had to be brought to their knees by many misfortunes. Pestilence raged in Prague. Thousands of persons died, among them some monks, and the Prior himself nearly died.

When his attention was called to the miraculous image, he vowed to spread its devotion if he would be cured. Shortly thereafter the Prior ordered a general devotion to the Infant, in which all the friars took part. Thus the Infant won the hearts of the Carmel of Prague, and became the cornerstone of their devotion.

Later the statue was brought into the church, so that the people at large might take part in its veneration. Daniel Wolf was a benefactor for its first shrine.

Other Propagators of the Devotion

THE cure of Baroness Elizabeth Kolowrat, in 1639, was another impetus in spreading the devotion. She had a crown of pure gold made for her great "Heavenly Physician," the miraculous Infant. Her husband gave rich alms to the Carmelites as long as he lived, and in his will left to the miraculous statue, among other things, a silver lamp and costly reliquary.

In 1641 this lady donated three thousand florins for the erection of an altar to the Blessed Trinity, with a magnificently gilded tabernacle as the resting-place for the miraculous statue, when exposed for public veneration. Subsequently numerous favors were attributed to the Infant, and votive offerings increased greatly.

Another lady, Febronia Perstyn, took care of beautifying the presbytery of the church with five red and white marble slabs, and another lady named Brunetta founded the perpetual light before the statue.

In 1642 Baroness Benigna Lobkowitz financed the erection of a handsome chapel for the Infant, which was blessed in 1644 on the feast of the Most Holy Name of Jesus. This has remained the principal feastday of the miraculous Infant ever since. The Baroness Eusebia Pernstyn, in gratitude for winning a lawsuit regarding her estate in Solnice,

Bohemia, became a generous benefactor to all projects relating to the Infant.

Ecclesiastical Approval

THE first ecclesiastical approval of the devotion was given by Ernest Cardinal Harrach, Archbishop of Prague, when on the third of May 1648 he consecrated the chapel and gave permission to all priests, secular and regular, to say Mass on the altar. In 1651 the Carmelite general, Father Francis of the Blessed Sacrament, made a canonical visitation to the monastery to examine matters regarding the devotion.

As a result, he issued a special decree approving the devotion, ending a controversy among the Carmelites themselves, and making it clear that the devotion is providential to the spiritual benefit of all devotees. On April 4, 1655 the Infant of Prague was solemnly crowned and proclaimed as a King.

Count Ignatius Martinic provided a golden crown, and a liturgical ceremony was performed by the auxiliary bishop of Prague, Joseph de Corti, in the name of Cardinal Harrach himself. Thus the devotion to the Infant of Prague was specified as the devotion to the Infant King, to be differentiated from the Babe of Bethlehem.

Spontaneous popular acceptance of the Infant King resulted in the fact that the final magnificent shrine, called the Talmberg Chapel after its benefactors, was established in 1741, on the epistle side of the church of Our Lady of Victory. It became one of the most famous in the world.

At the same time the royal representation of the Infant King became the devotional trademark by which the Infant of Prague fascinated the whole world. The title of "miraculous" came from the abundance of granted favors, for various human needs and to people in all walks of life.

It is evident that the devotion to the Infant of Prague stands firmly on the ground of canonical and ecclesiastical requirements, rising steadily from the need of the faithful to become subjects of the Great King of Kings, and to fulfill the historic mission—the spiritual rebirth of the people.

Universal Appeal of This Devotion

THIS is why the amazing story of the Infant of Prague has such universal appeal; why, as time passes, His statue adorns practically every Catholic church, convent, monastery, and home; and why His devotees are richly rewarded for heeding literally His promise: "The more you honor Me, the more I will bless you!"

The Carmelites made this devotion a part of their apostolate, and its spread was accelerated by a decree of the Carmelite Austrian Province in 1739 ordering that all their converts have replicas of the statue, with the public devotions.

The popularity of the Little King of Prague spread to different countries in the eighteenth century. However it took quite some time before all corners of the continents could be reached. In the nineteenth century, the devotion was somewhat neglected because of the Enlightenment and anti-religious trends, until the time of Pope Leo XIII, who restored splendor to the Infant by confirming the Sodality of the Infant of Prague (1896) and granting many indulgences to the devotion to the Infant.

The twentieth century saw the great glory of the Infant of Prague, especially when Pope Pius X unified an organizing membership into a Confraternity under the guidance of the Carmelites.

Literary contributions in various languages, from sources such as popular histories, periodicals, and prayerbooks honoring the Infant of Prague, rapidly spread knowledge of the Little King. Devotionals, such as statues, medals, pictures, etc., reached such enormous proportions that statistics from leading religious stores and shops reveal the surprising fact that the Infant of Prague outsells all other devotionals of any kind. This is not only a proof of His tremendous popularity, but also a sign of the spiritual benefits experienced by devotees who know that the Little King of Prague is One, having all "power of heaven and earth!"

Venerable Father Cyril of the Mother of God, just promoter of the devotion to the Infant of Prague.

Part II
Patronages of the Infant of Prague

THE patronage of the Infant of Prague is the area of human problems in which the faithful are most benefited by honoring the Infant. Although there is no such word as "limit" when we speak of Divine Power, nevertheless history reveals, very faithfully, that the Infant's patronage was most effective everywhere.

1) Infant of Prague—Master of Vocations

THE first to witness the experience of the Infant as a Master of Vocations was Father Cyril of the Mother of God, the first promoter of this devotion, who found reassurances of his own religious vocation. The whole story of the statue itself is centered around this point. And it is logical that the Infant King takes good care of His servants, dedicated primarily to "seeking the kingdom of God."

This is why the religious Orders and Congregations have their monthly novenas, held from the sixteenth to the twenty-fifth of each month, for vocations. The diversity of such novenas, performed in different ways, indicates the spontaneous urge of all those who want to be one of the "chosen." The complexity of every vocation needs a special Divine patronage, because "being chosen" depends entirely on Divine choice.

2) Infant of Prague— Protector of Good Health

AS a vocation is the result of good spiritual health, it is reasonable that the principal interest of lay people is reflected in their desire for good physical health. The history of the devotion to the Infant reveals that among the first favors granted by Him were cures of illnesses.

All histories published about the Infant have listed so many unusual favors granted that one must know that the protection of the good health of the devotees is an integral part of His patronage. An early Carmelite historian, Father Emmerich, called Him "a Heavenly Physician."

It seems fitting to point out here that the modern devotion to the Holy Infant of Good Health, as it appears in Mexico (fostered by the Archbishop of Morelia), and in the Chicago area (fostered by the Fathers of the Divine Word), is similar in form to the devotion to the Infant as Protector of Good Health as seen in many other countries of the world.

The resemblance of these devotions indicates the popularity of the Infant of Prague as the Protector of Good Health. Many health resorts in European countries contain His statue, attesting to His title of "Heavenly Physician."

It is of special interest to stress the Infant of Prague as a protector of sick and retarded children. Children's institutions, orphanages, and adoption agencies, especially in the United States, accepted the Infant of Prague as their powerful patron. The early history of the devotion emphasizes how sick children enjoyed His favors.

Spiritually and psychologically, this approach to the Infant in regard to children reflects Christ's tenderness to them as depicted in Holy Scripture. The most helpless are entitled and privileged to have the greatest help, indeed.

In recent years, the Infant of Prague was accepted by those stricken with polio, paralysis, cancer, arthritis, and other crippling diseases. He became their favorite protector. In the Chicago and New York metropolises, especially, patients in practically every hospital and rehabilitation center enjoy the presence of the statue of the Infant, and revel in devotion to Him. Research in this direction is very convincing on this point.

3) Infant of Prague—Good Financier

AMONG the most frequent problems in everyone's life is material welfare. Indeed there are situations of financial worries and troubles that seem beyond human hope. In this regard there is the inspiring story of the repair of the statue, showing how the Infant of Prague was so helpful in human need.

The Discalced Carmelites in Prague made Him the Master of the house, and trusted Him to make the administration of their monastery a prosperous one. This became an inspiration to other Orders and Congregations, which accepted Him as their Good Provider. In some places the Infant of Prague was selected as a Protector of church or school buildings, or Protector of financial projects, and He never let His benefactors become discouraged.

Some of His devotees anxiously put coins or checks for the desired sums under the statue, while making novenas honoring the Infant. He seemed even to make the practical mind of the anxious find ways of regulating their business. Devotionals of the Infant are distributed in business circles in the hope of securing success.

This idea of putting business on the basis of moral standards with honesty and dignity, instead of mutual exploitation, is to be highly recommended, and there is nothing superstitious in seeking Divine blessing for honest efforts.

4) Infant of Prague—Refuge of Families

FROM the start of the devotion the people of Prague brought replicas of the miraculous statue to their homes and consecrated themselves to the Infant. Gradually pictures and statues of the Infant found their way into the majority of homes on every continent. Indeed, the original statue was a family treasure of Maria Manriquez de Lara, indicating that the home was meant to be the first place to honor the Infant.

The modern motto: "The family that prays together stays together," is becoming more effective before the statue of the Infant. The education and rearing of children in "age, wisdom and grace" is considered the most important function of parents. No wonder then that they select the Infant Who excels in these very virtues which should be reflected in all children.

5) Infant of Prague—Delight of Children

CHILDREN enjoy a special Divine protection. In Holy Scripture, Jesus speaks: "Let the little children come to Me." Apostolates of children have the special patronage of the Infant, and schools as well as all other children's institutions, orphanages, hospitals, adoption agencies and other educational centers for children have His statue in their abodes, with the practice of the proper devotion. The tenderness which radiates through the statue is exceptionally influential on the souls of children, and they experience complete security under His protection.

6) Infant of Prague—Patron of Schools

IT IS in connection with one's individual freedom that schools enjoy a special patronage of the Infant of Prague. So it is in schools where children feel free to reach the real truth in all the fields of human knowledge, since Jesus is "The Way, The Truth, and The Life."

Lessons derived from the Holy Infancy can be endorsed by these little practical reminders:

   a) To have a statue in every classroom.
   b) To accept the Holy Child of Prague as an example of right growing.

c) To learn to wear a little medal and to pray the little Rosary to the Infant.

d) To exercise monthly, on the 25th day, the consecration of youth to the Infant, placing oneself under His protection.

The same should be applied to the different clubs and cultural associations, or wherever youth is in the process of learning.

7) Infant of Prague—Prince of Peace

THE people of Prague very often experienced a special protection of the Infant in the turbulent years of the Thirty Years' War (1618-1648), and, as Father Emmerich in his German biography stressed, they called Him "Prince of Peace." In gratitude for His wondrous solution to the many complicated political situations, the people of Prague proclaimed Him a King and on many occasions expressed it in tangible ways.

Symbolically, the Infant's desire for world peace is expressed when He holds the whole world in His hand. In modern times, when the entire orbit is threatened by destructive nuclear weapons, and everlasting peace is much to be desired for the sake of every nation, His Patronage, as Prince of Peace, is needed more than ever.

"Peace to men of good will" was indeed the first message at the Bethlehem scene, showing clearly and implicitly how this role of Prince of Peace is a precise and ever-expressive interpretation of His mission. Furthermore, the Holy Child as King is ever an impressive reminder to all those frequently appearing dictators in history that not titans but little ones are pleasing to God.

8) Infant of Prague—Source of Freedom

THE human being was endowed by the Creator with the dignity of being free. Only the free being can select his eternal destiny. However, human relationship, or society, sometimes deprives the human being of his freedom in order to achieve its goal of collective security. Pressure on society or state often creates a situation where individual freedom and expression is limited, or even denied, suspending human rights and the pursuit of happiness.

It is evident that only under the banner of Christ the King can human beings enjoy their freedom, and subsequently He hears all those who plead for their freedom, even while in chains of slavery. It is interesting to note that all dictators in the history of mankind were, first of all, oppressors of religious freedom, primarily because of the above-mentioned reasons.

9) Infant of Prague—Helper of Missions

TO gain souls for Christ is to enlarge the Kingdom of God, and the Infant of Prague was accepted as the Helper of Missions. It is indeed the proper task of Christ the King to patronize every effort to save souls for His kingdom. Therefore it is not accidental that missionaries take a statue with them and place their missions under His protection. It was because of their efforts that the devotion to the Infant reached such widespread proportions in such a short time in all the continents of the world.

The foregoing patronages attributed to the Infant of Prague's special care are mentioned because they appear in historical records and in the constant flow of prayers throughout the centuries. This does not mean, however, that other areas of human need are not included in His loving care.

On the contrary. Such an impressive representation of the Son of God, Savior and Redeemer, in the appearance of the Holy Child, reveals Him so that any problem can be placed in His care in the hope of being heard. A childlike approach of putting complete confidence in the Infant seems to be the greatest mystery which emanates from the devotion.

Further, the fact that Divine Blessing is assured with the expected honor, as it is expressed in that historical promise: "The more you honor Me, the more I will bless you!" excludes any doubt as to whether the Infant would hear any need. However, there are these two factors: complete confidence and the will to honor the Infant, which are the keys for everyone to the treasury of the Infant's favors.

10) Infant of Prague—Protector of Safety

THE attribute is of rather recent date. The tremendous popularity of the Infant of Prague found its way also into the transportation field, like that of plane, train, and especially automobiles. One can find His little statue, medals, or stickers, in many modern cars, as a symbol expressing Him as the Protector of Safety on busy highways and turnpikes where the danger of accidents appears to be quite frequent. The practice of putting ourselves under the powerful protection of the Miraculous Infant of Prague to prevent sudden death is to be much recommended, since He as the Son of God insures our eternal salvation under all circumstances.

It seems coincidental, but this case which I experienced is true. In 1956 I was on my way to New York from Bridgeport, Connecticut, and although I had a train ticket, I was walking to reach my destination. I had a two-hour wait on the train, and something seemed to tell me not to waste my time there. While on the road I heard a terrible noise, and a stranger told me there was a collision up ahead. I ran to the scene, reaching in my pocket for the stole that I always carry with me. While the ambulances were coming, I ministered to all the injured.

Three cars were involved. But what I shall never forget is the fact that in the third car was a statue of the Infant of Prague. After I finally administered the Last Rites in that car, I was removing my stole when I glanced at the statue on the dashboard, and then I noticed a little piece of paper before it which read "In case of an accident, Dear Infant, please see that a priest is nearby." All persons involved in this accident, although seriously injured, recovered.

Statue of the Holy Child robed in royal vestments.

Part III
Spiritual Treasury of the Devotion

Statutes of the Confraternity of the Holy Child Jesus of Prague
(Sacred Cong. of the Council, July 24, 1913, and "Rescript," Feb. 17, 1923)

A. Purpose of the Confraternity

1. Promote worship of the Holy Child Jesus; propose to the pious meditation of the faithful, and particularly of the Associates, the example of His hidden life and His ineffable virtues, in order to imitate them; obtaining thus, that their hearts become more and more inflamed with love toward the Incarnate Word.

2. Place all Associates, and especially the children, under the particular protection of the Holy Child Jesus, so that, thanks to the abundance of His blessings, He protects their innocence and preserves them from the snares and the corruption of the world.

B. Administration and Exercises of the Confraternity

1. The Director of the Confraternity will be the Rector of the church or chapel of the Carmelite Order in which the Confraternity is erected. For the churches or chapels which do not belong to this

Order, the appointment of the Director will be submitted to the approval of the Ordinary.

2. The money which might be offered spontaneously by the Associates will be entirely used for the increase of the sacred worship, or sent to the missions for the ransom of pagan children.

3. On the 25th of each month, or on another day specified, a pious exercise in honor of the Divine Child Jesus will take place in the church or chapel of the Confraternity.

4. The annual festivity of the Confraternity, affixed to the 1st Sunday after the Circumcision, or at any other day to be specified once and for all, will be celebrated with solemnity.

C. Obligation of the Members

1. Give their name, in order to be registered at the Confraternity in the book.

2. Wear around the neck or any other suitable place the medal of the Divine Child Jesus, blessed and laid on at the reception ceremony, by the priest empowered to do so.

3. Recite daily 3 times the "Glory be to the Father" with the ejaculatory prayer: "Divine Child Jesus, bless me."

D. Pious Exercises Recommended to the Members

1. Participate with pious care in the devotions taking place in honor of the Divine Child Jesus in

the church or chapel of the Confraternity on the 25th of each month, or on some other day specified, as well as on the solemnity of the annual festivity.

2. Receive frequently, if age permits it, the sacraments of Penance and the Holy Eucharist, especially on the Feastday of Our Lord and on the day of the regular monthly devotion.

Almost every country has so-called National Shrines of the Infant of Prague with National Headquarters for the devotion to the Infant, which are helpful in its promotion. Where the Confraternity is not yet established or not yet desired, it is advisable for the devotees to register at the nearest National Headquarters.

Devotional Exercises

FROM the beginning of the devotion to the Infant of Prague, a Feast of the Most Holy Name of Jesus was an annual feast, originally affixed to January 14, but later extended to the 2nd Sunday after the Epiphany by Pope Innocent XIII in 1721. Pius X affixed it to the Sunday between the Circumcision and Epiphany, or January 2, if there be no coincidence of feasts. In that case, the external celebration of the Solemn Mass could be transferred to the 2nd Sunday after the Epiphany.

The Statutes of the Confraternity favor this custom; nevertheless they give an opportunity of celebrating the Confraternity's feast on some other suitable day by the utilization of a privilege to say a votive Mass from the Feast of the Most Holy Name of Jesus.

It is recommended that all members of the Confraternity keep the annual Feast of the Most Holy Name of Jesus by receiving the Sacraments, and participating in the appropriate devotions or novenas in church, or in the Confraternity's Chapel.

There is a monthly Feast of the Confraternity on the 25th of every month, in commemoration of the Nativity of our Savior. Although the nature of this devotion is not determined, it is intended to remind the members of the mysteries of the Holy Infancy. By the statutes of the Confraternity it is recommended to the members to receive the Sacraments, if age permits, and to participate in the customary devotion for this occasion.

In some countries, the different Carmelite centers have a pious exercise in honor of the mysteries of the Infancy of our Lord Jesus Christ which takes place on twelve successive Sundays of the year.

In addition to these official days of the Confraternity there are many pious exercises, which are held on the congregation's level, or on personal ones. The weekly devotion grew to great popularity. Which day is to be selected depends on the Rector of the Church, or on some favored day accepted by established tradition. The program of these weekly devotions varies. Usually it consists of devotional services and Benediction. In some places a blessing of children is a part of it.

In some countries, as in Italy (Arenzano), a special day of the year, such as the first Sunday in September, is reserved for this blessing. Pious exercises on personal levels differ: some devotees recite the so-called storm novenas—every hour of the day a short prayer for some special need; other devotees say an obligatory prayer prescribed by the Confraternity, consisting of short invocations for the Infant's blessing.

A special place in the devotion is reserved for the novenas, whether they are annual, monthly, weekly, daily, or hourly novenas. While the daily or hourly novena depends upon one's personal choice, weekly, monthly or annual novenas are usually conducted by the congregation. An important place is occupied by the monthly novenas in convents, called vocation novenas.

All these devotional practices are so manifold that it is not easy to find desired uniformity in them. The diversity of devotional and novena booklets, used by various churches, reveal only certain favorite prayers or hymns, but definitely indicate the popularity of the devotion to the Infant with its strong appeal to the people.

Blessing of School Children

IN many countries, the special day of this blessing is usually the first Sunday in September. However, it can be another suitable day.

The priest, vested in surplice and stole, turning toward the children, prays:

℣. Our help is in the name of the Lord.
℟. **Who made heaven and earth.**

Ant. Praise the Lord, you children, praise
the name of the Lord.

Praise the Lord, you children,
  praise the name of the Lord.
Blessed be the name of the Lord
  both now and forever.
From the rising to the setting of the sun
  is the name of the Lord to be praised.
High above all nations is the Lord,
  above the heavens is His glory.
Who is like the Lord, our God, Who is enthroned
    on high
  and looks upon the heavens and the earth below?
He raises up the lowly from the dust;
  from the dunghill He lifts up the poor
To seat them with princes,
  with the princes of His own people.
He establishes in her home the barren wife
  as the joyful mother of children.
  Glory be to the Father, etc.

The Antiphon is repeated:

Ant. Praise the Lord, you children, praise the
  name of the Lord.

The priest then continues:

℣. Suffer the little children to come to Me.
℟. **For of such is the kingdom of heaven.**

℣. Their angels
℟. **Always behold the face of the Father.**
℣. Let not the enemy prevail against them.
℟. **Nor the son of iniquity draw near to hurt them.**
℣. O Lord, hear my prayer.
℟. **And let my cry come to You.**
℣. The Lord be with you.
℟. **And also with you.**

Let us pray. O Lord Jesus, You embraced children who were brought to You. Placing Your hands on them, You blessed them, saying: "Let the children come to Me and do not hinder them. It is to such as them that the kingdom of God belongs," and "their angels in heaven constantly behold My Father's face."

Look upon the innocence of these little ones and the devotion of their parents and graciously bless them through our ministry. Help them to grow in knowledge and love of You, serve You faithfully by keeping Your commandments, and attain their desired goal. You live and reign with God the Father and the Holy Spirit for ever and ever. ℟. **Amen.**

Let us pray. Lord, through the intercession of the Blessed Virgin Mary defend this family from all adversity. As they kneel humbly before You, protect them against all the snares of the enemy. We ask this through Christ our Lord. ℟. **Amen.**

Let us pray. God, in Your providence You saw fit to send Your angels to watch over us. Grant that we may always be under their protection and one day enjoy their company in heaven. We ask this through Christ our Lord. ℟. **Amen.**

Then the priest blesses the children in the form of a cross, saying:

May God, the Father, the Son, and the Holy Spirit, bless you and keep your hearts and your minds. ℟. **Amen.**

He then sprinkles them with holy water. A homily and the consecration of the children follows. Benediction closes the ceremony.

Children's Consecration Prayer to the Infant of Prague

MIRACULOUS Infant Jesus, I acknowledge You as my beloved Little King and adore You. Establish Your reign in my heart and in the hearts of all men. Thank You for the countless graces and blessings bestowed upon the whole world. Forgive the many offenses committed against Your Divine Majesty, and accept this act of homage and love which I offer You in reparation for my sins and the sins of others.

Teach me to be meek and humble of heart, to be docile and subject to all those who exercise authority over me in Your name, that I may grow in wisdom, age, and grace before God and men. Instill in my heart those childlike virtues of simplicity and candor, humility and trust, so necessary for entrance into the kingdom of heaven. Make me strong in the face of temptation, and pure in my thoughts, desires, words and actions.

Keep me steadfast and loyal in Your service and that of Your Church, faithful to the ideals of my country, my home, and my school. Give me a love for learning and an appreciation of the good and beautiful. Keep me honorable and generous in my dealings with others. Grant me a reverence and respect for the priesthood and bless all those who serve You in this exalted calling.

Bless my parents and relatives, my teachers and classmates, and all those to whom I am indebted in any way. Bless all children, especially those who suffer privation and pain. Bless, dearest Jesus, the days of my youth, that they may prove profitable for eternity. And finally when the shadows lengthen on the close of my days, may Your tiny hand, lifted in familiar benediction, trace over me a last blessing, and may Your promise to bless those who honor You be the source of my hope and consolation.

O Miraculous Infant Jesus of Prague, You promised "The more you honor Me, the more I will bless you." Grant that I and all those near and dear to me may know happy fulfillment.

Chaplet of the Infant of Prague

THE origin, as well as the practice, of this chaplet, called Little Crown, stems from Venerable Sister Margaret of the Blessed Sacrament, Carmelite Sister of the Beaune Carmel, who died in 1648. This chaplet is composed of fifteen beads in such a way that three beads are in honor of the Holy Family: Jesus, Mary and Joseph. On these are recited three times the Lord's Prayer. The twelve other beads are in honor of the Holy Childhood of Christ, and on them are recited twelve Hail Marys. Before each Lord's Prayer one says: "And the Word was made Flesh." Before the first of the twelve Hail Marys one prays: "And the Word was made Flesh, and dwelt among us."

The Coronation of the Infant of Prague

THE crowning of replicas of the Infant of Prague in some countries, including annual anniversaries, stems from the first solemn Coronation of the Infant (April 5, 1655). However there is no established tradition of rites for such a coronation. Its purpose is rather to give a solemnity to the fact that the Infant of Prague represents the King of the world. Suitability of time depends on the Rector of the church; the most appropriate time, however, would be the Feast of the Most Holy Name of Jesus, or of Christ the King.

The different ways of conducting such a coronation reveal only that a triduum or novena appears to be a fitting preparation for the occasion, climaxed with the consecration of the people to the Infant King, during Benediction services. Application of prayers differs; nevertheless prayers of the consecration of Christ the King can be recommended.

Prayer to Christ the King

O Christ Jesus, I acknowledge You King of the Universe. All that has been created has been made for You. Exercise upon me all Your rights. I renew my baptismal promises, renouncing Satan and all his works and pomps. I promise to live a good Christian life and to do all in my power to procure the triumph of the rights of God and Your Church.

Divine Heart of Jesus, I offer You my poor actions in order to obtain that all hearts may acknowledge Your sacred Royalty, and that thus the reign of Your peace may be established throughout the universe. Amen.

Coronation Hymn

O Jesus King, we crown Thee
  With diadem most fair.
O'er all Thou reignest solely.
  Thy might is everywhere.
With pride we tell Thy story,
  O Wondrous Babe of Prague!
With joy we sing Thy glory,
  O Little King of Prague!

Aspirations

The aspirations to Christ the King seem most suitable. They follow.

Jesus, King and center of all hearts, by the coming of Your kingdom, grant us peace.

Christ conquers! Christ reigns! Christ commands!

The statue of the Holy Child is dressed in the priest's alb. Over this royal robes are worn.

Part IV
Historical Prayers

IT is certain that the historical prayers, inspired by the first promoter of this devotion, Venerable Father Cyril of the Mother of God, and used in the Shrine of the Infant of Our Lady of Victory Church of Prague, are of the utmost importance, revealing the basic characteristics of the devotion to the Infant King.

Aspirations of Venerable Father Cyril

MY JESUS, Holy Child, I love in Thee
The Son of God and of the Virgin Mary;
I pray, from present needs deliver me:
For truly do I firmly trust in Thee
That Thou as God canst provide for me.
Wherefore, confidently, I place my hope in Thee
That Thy favors will be granted to me.
Hence with heart and soul I cherish Thee;
Sorrow for my sins deeply grieves me.
Because of them humbly I beseech Thee,
O Jesus, to root them out completely.
I promise never more to offend Thee,
And therefore, Jesus, surrender all to Thee.
My neighbor as myself I love for Thee.
Most powerful Jesus, hear my prayerful plea
To suffer and to serve Thee faithfully,
And I adore and worship Thee accordingly.

Deliver me from this necessity:
That with the Virgin Mother, worthily
Like Joseph and Teresa virgin, Thee
We may enjoy with heaven's court eternally.
O my Jesus, Jesus, dearest Jesus,
Have mercy on us. Amen! Amen! Amen!

Father Cyril's Prayers to the Infant

JESUS, unto Thee I flee,
Through Thy Mother, praying Thee
In my need to succor me.
Truly I believe of Thee;
God Thou art, with strength to shield me;
Full of trust I hope in Thee.
Thy grace Thou wilt give me;
And all my heart I yield Thee.
For my sins I repent me;
From their guilt, I beseech Thee,
And from their bondage free me.
Firm my purpose to mend me,
Never again to grieve Thee.
Unto Thee I give me wholly,
Patiently to suffer for Thee
And serve Thee faithfully.
My neighbor too, like to me,
I will love for love of Thee.
Little Jesus, I fondly pray Thee
In all my needs to aid me,
That one day I may enjoy Thee,
Safe with Joseph and with Mary
And angels all, eternally. Amen.

Litany of the Most Holy Name of Jesus

L ORD, have mercy.
Christ, have mercy.
Lord, have mercy.
Christ, hear us
Christ, graciously hear us.
God, the Father of heaven, **have mercy on us!**
God, the Son, Redeemer of the world, . . .
God the Holy Spirit,
Holy Trinity, one God,
Jesus, Son of the living God,
Jesus, Son of the Virgin Mary,
Jesus, mighty God,
Jesus, most powerful,
Jesus, most perfect,
Jesus, most worthy of praise,
Jesus, most wonderful,
Jesus, most lovable,
Jesus, most loving,
Jesus, brighter than the stars,
Jesus, more beautiful than the moon,
Jesus, brighter than the sun,
Jesus, most humble,
Jesus, most mild,
Jesus, most patient,
Jesus, most sweet
Jesus, lover of chastity,
Jesus, our joy and our love,
Jesus, King of peace,
Jesus, Mirror of the interior life,
Jesus, Example of all virtues,

Jesus, zealous for souls, **have mercy on us!**
Jesus, our Refuge, . . .
Jesus, Father of the poor,
Jesus, Comforter of the afflicted,
Jesus, Treasure of the faithful,
Jesus, a precious Gem,
Jesus, a Treasury of perfection,
Jesus, good Shepherd,
Jesus, Star of the sea,
Jesus, true Light of the world,
Jesus, eternal Wisdom,
Jesus, infinite Goodness,
Jesus, Joy of angels,
Jesus, King of patriarchs,
Jesus, Ruler of prophets,
Jesus, Ruler of Apostles,
Jesus, Teacher of evangelists,
Jesus, Strength of martyrs,
Jesus, Light of confessors,
Jesus, Spouse of virgins,
Jesus, Crown of all saints,
Be merciful, **spare us, O Jesus.**
Be merciful, **deliver us, O Jesus.**
From all evil, **deliver us, O Jesus.**
From all sin, . . .
From Your wrath,
From the snares of the devil,
From the transgression of Your Commandments,
From the attack of all enemies,
Through Your holy Incarnation,
Through Your holy Coming,
Through Your holy Birth,

Through Your holy Circumcision,
Through Your pain and labor, **deliver us, O Jesus.**
Through Your scourging, . . .
Through Your holy death,
Through Your holy Resurrection,
Through Your holy Ascension,
Through Your holy Coronation,
Through Your glory,
Through the intercession of Your holy Mother and Virgin,
Through the intercession of all the Saints,
Lamb of God, Who take away the sins of the world, **spare us, O Lord!**
Lamb of God, Who take away the sins of the world, **graciously hear us, O Lord!**
Lamb of God, Who take away the sins of the world, **have mercy on us, O Lord!**

℣. Jesus, hear us.
℟. **Jesus, graciously hear us.**

Our Father . . .
℣. Lord, hear my prayer.
℟. **And let my cry come to You.**

Let us pray. O almighty and eternal God, through the glorious Name of Your dear Son, our Lord Jesus Christ, You filled the hearts of the faithful with the greatest consolation and sweetness and have made the evil spirit fear and tremble. Grant that all who devoutly honor the Holy Name of Jesus may attain the unspeakable joy and bliss of heaven. We ask this through Christ our Lord. ℟. **Amen.**

℣. The Name of the Lord be praised.
℟. **Both now and forever.**

Litany of the Infant Jesus
(For Private Devotion)

LORD, have mercy.
Christ, have mercy.
Lord, have mercy.
Jesus, hear us.
Jesus, graciously hear us.
God the Father of heaven, **have mercy on us.**
God, the Son, Redeemer of the world, . . .
God, the Holy Spirit,
Holy Trinity, one God,
Infant, Jesus Christ,
Infant, true God,
Infant, Son of the living God,
Infant, Son of the Virgin Mary,
Infant, strong in weakness,
Infant, powerful in tenderness,
Infant, treasure of grace,
Infant, fountain of love,
Infant, renewer of the heavens,
Infant, repairer of the evils of earth,
Infant, head of the angels,
Infant, root of the patriarchs,
Infant, speech of prophets,
Infant, desire of the Gentiles,
Infant, joy of shepherds,
Infant, light of the Magi,
Infant, salvation of infants,
Infant, expectation of the just,

Infant, instructor of the wise, **have mercy on us.**

Infant, first-fruits of all saints, **have mercy on us.**

Be merciful, **spare us, O Infant Jesus.**

Be merciful, **graciously hear us, O Infant Jesus.**

From the slavery of the children of Adam, **Infant Jesus, deliver us.**

From the slavery of the devil, . . .

From the evil desires of the flesh,

From the malice of the world,

From the pride of life,

From the inordinate desire of knowing,

From the blindness of spirit,

From an evil will,

From our sins,

Through Your most pure Conception,

Through Your most humble Nativity,

Through Your tears,

Through Your most painful Circumcision,

Through Your most glorious Epiphany,

Through Your most pious Presentation,

Through Your most Divine life,

Through Your poverty,

Through Your many sufferings,

Through Your labors and travels,

Lamb of God, Who take away the sins of the world, **have mercy on us, O Infant Jesus.**

Lamb of God, Who take away sins of the world, **graciously hear us, O Infant Jesus.**

Lamb of God, Who take away the sins of the world, **have mercy on us, O Infant Jesus.**

℣. Jesus, Infant, hear us.

℞. **Jesus, Infant, graciously hear us.**

Let us pray. O Lord Christ, You were pleased so to humble Yourself in Your incarnate Divinity and most sacred Humanity as to be born in time and become a little child. Grant that we may acknowledge infinite wisdom in the silence of a child, power in weakness, and majesty in humiliation. Adoring Your humiliations on earth, may we contemplate Your glories in heaven, Who with the Father and the Holy Spirit live and reign forever. R℟. **Amen.**

Litany to the Miraculous Infant of Prague
(For Private Devotion)

L ORD, have mercy.
Christ, have mercy.
Lord, have mercy.
Christ, hear us.
Christ, graciously hear us.
God the Father of heaven, **have mercy on us.**
God the Son, Redeemer of the world, . . .
God the Holy Spirit,
Holy Trinity, one God,
O merciful Infant Jesus,
O Infant Jesus, true God,
O Infant Jesus . . .
Whose omnipotence is shown in miracles, **have mercy on us.**
Whose wisdom searches our heart and mind,
Whose kindness is ever ready to send us aid,
Whose providence leads us to our final end,
Whose truth brightens the darkness of our hearts,
Whose generosity enriches the poor, **have mercy on us.**

Whose friendliness is comfort to the sad of heart, . . .

Whose mercy forgives the sins of men,

Whose power protects us from harm,

Whose justice deters us from evil,

Whose power overpowers hell,

Whose lovely image draws our hearts and minds,

Whose magnificence embraces the entire world with His hand,

Whose heart aflame with love enkindles our cold hearts,

Whose outstretched little hand of mercy fills us with heavenly bliss,

Whose sweetest and most holy Name is joy to all who believe in Christ

Whose glory fills all the world,

Be merciful, **spare us, O Infant Jesus!**

Be merciful, **hear us, O Infant Jesus!**

From all evil, **deliver us, O Infant Jesus!**

From all sin, . . .

From all distrust of Your unending kindness,

From all doubts about Your miraculous power,

From all lukewarm efforts to worship You,

From all want and need,

By all the mysteries of Your Holy Childhood,

We poor sinners pray to You, **hear us.**

Through the help of Mary, Your Virgin Mother and Joseph, Your foster father, **please hear us.**

That You forgive our sins, we pray . . .

That You absolve us from punishment for our sins,

That You may enrich and preserve our love for worship of Your holy Infancy,

That You never retract Your merciful hand from us, **please hear us.**

That You keep us eternally grateful for the many graces we have received, . . .

That You move us more and more to love Your Divine Heart,

That You may hear all who come to You in need with faith,

That You may preserve peace for our country,

That You may deliver us from any evil that threatens us,

That You repay those with eternal life who are generous toward You,

That You grant us blessings at the hour of death,

That You be merciful to us on judgment day,

That You remain our comfort through Your holy image, **we pray You, please hear us.**

Jesus, Son of God and holy Mary, **hear us, we pray.**

Lamb of God, Who take away the sins of the world, **spare us, O Infant Jesus!**

Lamb of God, Who take away the sins of the world, **graciously hear us, O Infant Jesus!**

Lamb of God, Who take away the sins of the world, **have mercy on us, O Infant Jesus!**

℣. Infant Jesus, hear us!

℟. **Infant Jesus, graciously hear us.**

Our Father . . .

Let us pray. O merciful Infant Jesus, we kneel before Your holy image and pray that You may cast Your merciful eye upon our anxious and beseeching hearts. Let our prayers soften Your compassionate heart and grant us the favors for which we pray from the depth of our hearts.

Take from us all sadness and despair, all want and need that burden us. In the name of Your holy Childhood, let us find help and send us comfort through the Father and the Holy Spirit forever and ever. ℟. **Amen.**

Litany Honoring the Holy Childhood of Jesus

(For Private Devotion)

Lord, have mercy.
Christ, have mercy.
Lord, have mercy.
Christ, hear us.
Christ, graciously hear us.
God the Father in heaven, **have mercy on us.**
God the Son, Redeemer of the world, . . .
God the Holy Spirit,
Holy Trinity, One God,
O Infant Jesus, sent to earth from heaven,
O divine Infant Jesus—
Born of Mary in Bethlehem,
Wrapped in swaddling clothes,
Placed in the crib,
Praised by the angels,
Adored by the shepherds,
Proclaimed as Savior through Your adorable Name,
Announced by the star,
Worshiped by the Magi with symbolic gifts,
Presented in the Temple by the Virgin,
Embraced by the aged Simeon,
Revealed in the Temple by the prophetess Anna,

Persecuted by King Herod, **have mercy on us.**
Fleeing into the exile of Egypt, . . .
Crowning with martyrdom the Infants of
  Bethlehem,
Rejoicing the heart of Mary with His first words,
Learning to take His first steps in exile,
Returning from Egypt to be reared in Nazareth,
Loved by all as a shining example of obedience,
Brought to the Temple at the age of twelve,
Lost by Mary and Joseph on their return home,
Sought for three days with great sorrow,
Found with great delight,
Be merciful, O Jesus,
Be merciful, **hear us, O Jesus!**
From all evil, **deliver us, O Jesus!**
From all sin, . . .
From misconduct in the Church,
From quarrels and anger,
From lies and thievery,
From evil talk and bad example,
From bad habits,
By Your Incarnation,
By Your birth,
By Your most bitter poverty,
By Your persecution and sufferings,
Through the intercession of Your most holy
  Mother,
Through the intercession of Your holy foster
  father,
Through the intercession of the Holy Innocents,
Through the intercession of all the angels and
  saints,

We, Your sinful children, **beseech You to hear us,**

Hear our prayer for the salvation of the unfortunate heathen, **we beseech You to hear us.**

With pity, . . .

That You may look benignly upon our small gifts,

That You number the men of God among Your Saints,

That You richly bless their apostolic works,

That all the world may kneel before You,

That we be zealous to convert all unbelievers, in the Name of Your Holy Childhood,

That we keep our Baptismal vows faithfully,

That we rejoice to be children of Your Father in heaven,

That we may ever honor and love our Father in heaven,

That we may pray as Christian children, freely and devoutly,

That we may willingly obey Your Commandments;

That we may inscribe in our heart the fourth Commandment: "Honor your father and your mother,"

That we may grow in wisdom and virtue as we grow in years,

That You may keep us innocent,

That You will deliver us from temptation,

That You may instill in us great love and devotion for Your Mother, Mary,

That we may never make an unworthy confession,

That we may receive Holy Communion with sincerity,

That You may grant our parents a long life, **we beseech You to hear us.**

That You may grant them Your best gifts, . . .

That You may enlighten our pastors and give them strength,

That You may repay our benefactors by eternal gifts,

That You may have mercy upon the poor souls in purgatory,

Lamb of God, Who take away the sins of the world, **spare us, O Lord!**

Lamb of God, Who take away the sins of the world, **hear our prayer, O Lord!**

Lamb of God, Who take away the sins of the world, **have mercy on us, O Lord!**

℣. Christ, hear us,

℟. **Christ, graciously hear us!**

Our Father . . .

Let us pray. We pray to You, heavenly Father, Who adopted us as His children and as heirs of heaven for the Infant Jesus' sake, that You may look kindly upon children not of the faith, and let them participate in our unearned and priceless fortune. We ask this through the Infant Jesus Christ, Your Son, our Lord, Who lives and reigns with You and the Holy Spirit forever and ever. ℟. **Amen.**

Prayer to the Most Loving Infant Jesus

O MOST loving and blessed Infant Jesus! great God and Lord of heaven and earth, You have hidden Your Divine Majesty under the lovable semblance of a child before Whom the powers of the heavens tremble, the mighty kings of the earth bow, and the evil spirits under the earth must bend. Though You are the Almighty God, for love of us You become a little Child, so that we might love You more ardently, serve You more faithfully, and humbly follow Your example in childlike purity and love.

I, a poor sinner, bow down humbly before the great God concealed in this lovable Child and adore You. I love You as the highest and most loving God. I entrust myself to Your infinite Goodness. Oh teach me after Your example to love humility and crush pride, to desire to grow in virtue and childlike trust. Direct and rule me and make me virtuous, that I may please You and be little in this world and great in the next. Amen.

Veneration of the Mysteries of the Holy Infancy

℣. O God, come to my assistance!
℟. **O Lord, make haste to help me!**
℣. Glory be to the Father, and to the Son, and to the Holy Spirit;
℟. **As it was in the beginning, is now, and ever shall be, world without end. Amen.**

Our Father . . .

I

JESUS, sweetest Child, You came down from the bosom of the Father for our salvation and were conceived by the Holy Spirit. You did not abhor the Virgin's womb, and, being the Word made flesh, took upon Yourself the form of a servant. Have mercy on us.

℟. **Have mercy on us, Child Jesus, have mercy on us.**

Hail Mary . . .

II

JESUS, sweetest Child, by means of Your Virgin Mother You visited Saint Elizabeth. You filled Your forerunner, John the Baptist, with Your Holy Spirit and sanctified him in his mother's womb. Have mercy on us.

℟. **Have mercy on us, Child Jesus, have mercy on us.**

Hail Mary . . .

III

JESUS, sweetest Child, You were enclosed for nine months in Your Mother's womb. During this time You were looked for with eager expectation by the Virgin Mary and Saint Joseph, and offered by God the Father for the salvation of the world. Have mercy on us.

℟. **Have mercy on us, Child Jesus, have mercy on us.**

Hail Mary . . .

IV

JESUS, sweetest Child, You were born in Bethlehem of the Virgin Mary, wrapped in swaddling clothes, and laid in a manger. You were announced by Angels and visited by shepherds. Have mercy on us.

℟. **Have mercy on us, Child Jesus, have mercy on us.**

Hail Mary . . .

All honor, laud and glory be,
O Jesus, Virgin-born, to Thee;
All glory, as is ever meet,
To Father and to Paraclete. Amen.

℣. Christ is near to us.
℟. **O Come, let us adore Him.**

Our Father . . .

V

JESUS, sweetest Child, You were wounded after eight days in Your circumcision and called by the glorious Name of Jesus. Thus, by Your Name and by Your blood You were foreshown as the Savior of the world. Have mercy on us.

℟. **Have mercy on us, Child Jesus, have mercy on us.**

Hail Mary . . .

VI

JESUS, sweetest Child, You were manifested by the leading of a star to the three Wise Men. You were worshiped in the arms of Your Mother and presented with the mystic gifts of gold, frankincense, and myrrh. Have mercy on us.

℟. **Have mercy on us, Child Jesus, have mercy on us.**

Hail Mary . . .

VII

JESUS, sweetest Child, You were presented in the Temple by Your Virgin Mother, taken up in Simeon's arms, and revealed to Israel by Anna, a prophetess. Have mercy on us.

℟. **Have mercy on us, Child Jesus, have mercy on us.**

Hail Mary . . .

VIII

JESUS, sweetest Child, You were sought by wicked Herod to be slain, and You were carried with Your Mother into Egypt by Saint Joseph. You were rescued from the cruel slaughter and You were glorified by the praises of the martyred Innocents. Have mercy on us.

℞. **Have mercy on us, Child Jesus, have mercy on us.**

Hail Mary . . .

All honor, laud and glory be,
O Jesus, Virgin-born, to Thee;
All glory, as is ever meet,
To Father and to Paraclete. Amen.

℣. Christ is near to us.
℞. **O come and let us worship.**

Our Father . . .

IX

JESUS, sweetest Child, You dwelt in Egypt with most holy Mary and the Patriarch, Saint Joseph, until the death of Herod. Have mercy on us.

℞. **Have mercy on us, Child Jesus, have mercy on us.**

Hail Mary . . .

X

JESUS, sweetest Child, You returned from Egypt to the land of Israel with Your parents, suffering many hardships on the way. You entered into the city of Nazareth. Have mercy on us.

℞. **Have mercy on us, Child Jesus, have mercy on us.**

Hail Mary . . .

XI

JESUS, sweetest Child, You dwelt most holily in the holy house at Nazareth, in subjection to Your parents. You were wearied by poverty and toil, and You increased in wisdom, age, and grace. Have mercy on us.

℟. **Have mercy on us, Child Jesus, have mercy on us.**

Hail Mary . . .

XII

JESUS, sweetest Child, You were brought to Jerusalem at twelve years of age. You were sought by Your parents sorrowing and found with joy after three days in the midst of the Doctors. Have mercy on us.

℟. **Have mercy on us, Child Jesus, have mercy on us.**

Hail Mary . . .

All honor, laud and glory be,
O Jesus, Virgin-born, to Thee;
All glory, as is ever meet,
To Father and to Paraclete. Amen.

(For Christmas Day and Its Octave)

℣. The Word was made flesh, alleluia.
℟. **And dwelt among us, alleluia.**

(For the Epiphany)

℣. Christ has manifested Himself to us, alleluia.
℟. **O come and let us worship, alleluia.**

(Throughout the Year)

℣. The Word was made flesh.
℟. **And dwelt among us.**

Let us pray. Almighty and everlasting God, Lord of heaven and earth, You revealed Yourself to little ones. Grant, we beg You, that we may venerate with due honor the sacred mysteries of Your Son, the Child Jesus, and copy them with due imitation. May we thus be enabled to enter the kingdom of heaven which You have promised to little children. Through the same Christ our Lord. Amen.

℣. The Word was made flesh.
℟. **And dwelt among us.**

Prayers for a Novena from the 16th to the 24th Day of Any Month

I. Eternal Father, I offer to Your honor and glory, for my eternal salvation and for the salvation of the whole world, the mystery of the birth of our Divine Redeemer.

Glory be to the Father . . .

II. Eternal Father, I offer to Your honor and glory, for my eternal salvation and for the salvation of the whole world, the sufferings of the most holy Virgin and Saint Joseph on that long and weary journey from Nazareth to Bethlehem, and the anguish of their hearts at not finding a place of shelter when the Savior of the world was about to be born.

Glory be to the Father . . .

III. Eternal Father, I offer to Your honor and glory, for my eternal salvation and for the salvation of the whole world, the suffering of Jesus in the manger where He was born, the cold He suffered, the tears He shed and His tender infant cries.

Glory be to the Father . . .

IV. Eternal Father, I offer to Your honor and glory, for my eternal salvation and for the salvation of the whole world, the pain which the Divine Child Jesus felt in His tender body, when He submitted to the rite of circumcision: I offer You that Precious Blood which He then first shed for the salvation of all mankind.

Glory be to the Father . . .

V. Eternal Father, I offer to Your honor and glory, for my eternal salvation and for the salvation of the whole world, the humility, mortification, patience, charity and all the virtues of the Child Jesus; I thank You, I love You, and I bless You infinitely for this ineffable mystery of the Incarnation of the Word of God.

Glory be to the Father . . .

℣. The Word was made flesh.
℟. **And dwelt among us.**

Let us pray. O God, Your only-begotten Son appeared in the substance of our flesh. Grant tha through Him Whom we acknowledge to have been outwardly like us, we may deserve to be renewed in our inward selves. He lives and reigns with You for ever and ever. Amen.

The Holy Child dressed in Chinese robes.

Part V
Prayers for All Occasions

Morning Prayer

HOLY Child, I believe in You; I hope in You; I love You with all my heart, my Infant Jesus.

I rise with You, my dear adorable Holy Child. Bless me and keep me from all evil of body and soul and protect me against all visible and invisible foes. O Jesus, I call to You in the early morning, for You are my God and my Lord, my Almighty Creator, my kind Savior and Redeemer. Just as Your holy angels visited You, O Holy Child Jesus, at the morning watch, and sing Your praise so I come to You, dear Infant Jesus, in the early morning hour, to praise and to honor and to hail You,

Hail, Heavenly Infant of mercy, I adore You. Manifold are the graces that come to us from the deep well of mercy overflowing with honey, that is Your Divine and sweet little heart. I thank You for having watched over me this last night and having given praise to Your heavenly Father on my behalf.

O beloved Infant Jesus of Prague, accept my poor unworthy heart as my morning sacrifice. I place it in Your heart with all the devotion I am capable of, and pray that You be merciful to me and stir me with Your love.

A Morning Offering to
the Holy Child

O DEAR, sweet Infant Jesus, I offer You: my will, that You strengthen it; my mind, that You inspire it; my memory, that You fill it; my wishes and desires, that You cleanse them. I sacrifice to You: my intentions, that You guide them; my trouble and my labor, that You bless them; all my inner and outer activities, that You make them sacred. All I am and all I have is Yours. Your love for me is my hope and my trust. Hear me and grant that I may never leave You. Amen.

O Infant Jesus, I form the belief that I shall be granted forgiveness of sins and place it into the hands of Your most Holy Mother Mary; I commend myself to all and every Holy Mass that is celebrated this day all over the globe, and I offer all this in behalf of the poor souls in purgatory.

(Resolve to fight your greatest evil today and to perform several acts of the opposite virtue because of your love for the Holy Child Jesus.)

Pledge of Love with the Holy Child

A LTHOUGH You are little in stature, You are still my Lord and God. Oh, that I could love You every hour of the day, from the bottom of my heart. Whatever I shall do, move a limb, or speak and think and act, the pulsing of my blood, the beating of my heart, it is because of love for You. Who calls for You so many times and offers his greatest love to You?

From the bottom of my heart I regret that so much time has passed. Forgive me, O most precious Infant, in the name of Your most precious blood. What could ever be against You, Jesus? Let death take me before I fall away again. Please, dear Jesus, say "Amen" as a seal for this pledge.

Evening Prayer

IN YOUR presence, O beloved, merciful Holy Child of Prague, I throw myself upon my knees and worship You in loving devotion. Oh, how much gratitude I owe to You! Not only did You save me from many dangers, but You also bestowed many graces upon me today. Thank You, thank You many times. Help me to recognize and be sorry for whatever wrong I did today and by which I might have saddened Your Divine Heart. Give me Your light and Your grace.

O Heart of my Savior, put in my heart the right understanding and repentance, the kind that will make it possible for You to give me again Your love and mercy and to enrich and strengthen it.

(Examination of conscience) Did I insult Jesus by my thoughts today? — In words, by deeds, by omissions? How did I fulfill my duties? Did I have

good intentions in all I did? Did I act against the will of God? Most of all, did I live up to my morning resolution?

Give ample thought to the reason that caused your downfall and find the means to protect yourself from falling in the future. Then repent according to the number of wrongs that you have committed and pray to God that He may strengthen and keep you.

I LOVE You, Infant Jesus, with all my heart.
And this imparts the deepest pain,
That I have irritated You.
Cleanse my heart within Your blood.
Impart to me the strongest will
That this should be my very last wrong.
And ready me to flee from sin
And to repent at any time.

Now, make the sign of the cross on your forehead and say: "Jesus, King of all nations, omnipotent Holy Child, save me, Your child and subject, from sudden death and all evil. Amen."

Night Commendation

INTO Your loving care, O Holy Child of Prague, I commend this night, my heart, my body and my soul. Protect them from danger and the pursuit of the evil foe. O dearest Infant Jesus, I am not able to praise You while I sleep; let Your Divine Heart replace what I miss. As long as my pulse shall beat, I shall praise the Blessed Trinity.

O Jesus, let me rest in this coming sleep as You have rested in the stable, upon straw, to the greatest pleasure of the heavenly Father. Dearest Infant Jesus, bless me. May I be blessed by God, the Father and the Son and the Holy Spirit, to Whom glory shall be forever.

Please accept me, Holy Child,
For I wish to be Your own,
Yours remaining while I'm living,
Yours alone, when I am dying;
Who shall serve You, King of the world,
Which entirely belongs to You?
My soul is Yours at any time.
With all my might I shall be Yours.
My body and my senses too
Shall never function without You;
With all my mind I shall endeavor
To think of you, now and forever.

O Holy Mary, Mother full of mercy and grace, Mother of my beloved Infant Jesus, protect me this night and in my last hour. Saint Joseph, powerful Patron of the Universal Church, be my protector also. Do not relinquish me in danger or in my prayers.

Angel of God, who are my guardian by the grace of the Lord, inspire and protect me; guide and lead me.

Lord, grant eternal peace to the souls of those who have passed before us and let eternal light shine upon them. May they rest in peace. Amen.

Dedication Prayer to the Infant of Prague

O DIVINE Infant Jesus, to You, Who love the handicapped, good, pious and eager children most, I dedicate myself today and consecrate the rest of my earthly life to the endeavor to please You, and to become more like You.

I solemnly resolve today to love You with all my heart and to do my best to follow more Your virtuous and inspiring examples. Help me to grow with age in wisdom, grace, virtue and piety. This I ask especially of You, that You preserve my innocence and the purity of my heart spotlessly. Amen.

A Prayer of a Child in Behalf of His Parents

DIVINE, merciful and miraculous Infant, I thank You that You have accepted me among those who adore You devoutly. Help me to be worthy of this grace forever and to remain a pious child that loves You with all his heart. Deliver me from sin and help me to serve You truly until my death.

Fill my heart with love and devotion toward my parents. Let me obey them with a happy heart and a willing mind and let me accept their admonitions and instructions without grumbling and obey them. O lovable Infant Jesus, return to them the kindness they are giving me, for I will never be able to return it all.

O Infant full of grace, bless my brothers and sisters besides me, that we may love one another sincerely, and grant us that we may worship You in heaven in time to come and praise You. Amen.

Short Personal Novena to the Little Infant

O CHILD Jesus, I have recourse to You by Your Holy Mother. I implore You to assist me in this need, for I firmly believe Your Divinity can assist me. I confidently hope to obtain Your holy grace. I love You with my whole heart and my whole soul. I am heartily sorry for my sins and beg of You, good Jesus, to give me strength to overcome them.

I make the resolution of never again offending You, and I resolve to suffer everything rather than displease You. Henceforth I will to serve You faithfully. For the love of You, Divine Child, I will love my neighbor as myself.

Jesus, most powerful Child, I implore You again to help me: *(mention your request)*.

Divine Child, great omnipotent God, I implore through Your most Holy Mother's most powerful intercession, and through the boundless mercy of Your omnipotence as God, a favorable answer to my prayer during this Novena.

Grant me the grace of possessing You eternally with Mary and Joseph and of adoring You with Your holy angels and saints. Amen.

To the Miraculous Infant of Prague

DEAREST Jesus, Little Infant of Prague, how tenderly You love us! Your greatest joy is to dwell among men and to bestow Your blessing upon us. Though I am not worthy that You should behold me, I feel drawn to You by love because

You are kind and merciful and exercise Your almighty power over me.

So many who turned to You with confidence have received graces and had their petitions granted. Behold me as I kneel before You and lay open my heart to You, with its prayers and hopes. I present to You especially this request, which I enclose in Your loving Heart: *(mention your request).*

Rule over me, dear Infant Jesus, and do with me and mine according to Your holy Will, for I know that in Your Divine wisdom and love You will arrange everything for the best. Do not withdraw Your hand from me, but protect and bless me forever.

I pray You, all-powerful and gracious Infant Jesus, for the sake of Your sacred infancy, in the name of Your Blessed Mother Mary who cared for You with such tenderness, and by the greatest reverence with which Saint Joseph carried You in his arms, help me in my needs. Make me truly happy with You, sweetest Infant, in time and in eternity, and I shall thank You forever with all my heart. Amen.

Almighty and Everlasting God, Lord of heaven and earth, You revealed Yourself to little ones. Grant, we beg of You, that we who venerate with due honor the sacred mysteries of Your Son, the Child Jesus, and imitate His example, may enter the kingdom of heaven which You have promised to little children. We ask this through Christ our Lord. Amen.

Pious Invocations

JESUS, friend of children, bless the children of the whole world.

———————

JESUS, Son of the living God, have mercy on us!
Jesus, Son of the Virgin Mary, have mercy on us.
Jesus, King and center of all hearts, grant that peace may be in Your kingdom.

———————

JESUS, with all my heart I cling to You.

———————

LORD Jesus, through Your infant cries when You were born for me in the manger, through Your love as You live for me in the tabernacle, have mercy on me and save me.

———————

MY JESUS, mercy.

———————

Front of the church of Our Lady of Victory
in Prague.

Part VI
Occasional Prayers to the Infant of Prague

Prayer of a Sick Person

O INFANT Jesus, full of grace! Your miracles for the sick are known to me. How many maladies did You cure while You were still upon earth! How many worshipers of this, Your holy Image, can thank You for their miraculous deliverance from the most severe, painful and hopeless illness!

I realize that a sinner like myself can bear no hope of ever receiving a miraculous cure and my suffering is just. Yet when I recall the many sinners who worshiped You by the adoration of Your infancy in this miraculous Image of Prague, or even in the veneration of pictures or statues of it, I have no fear and call to You.

O loving and merciful Infant of Prague, You have the power to heal me if You wish to do so. Do not prolong it, Divine Physician; if it is Your will that I shall recover from the present sickness, stretch out Your Divine little hands and take from me all pain and infirmity, for You are almighty. And please do so in such a way that I will have to ascribe my re-

covered health to You alone, not to natural re-
medies.

But if Divine plans are otherwise in Your infinite
wisdom, then at least help me to keep my soul in
grace, fill me with heavenly trust and comfort, and
make me like You, in further suffering. O my dear
Jesus, let me praise Your providence on my sick-
bed until it is Your will that I shall receive eternal
life by earthly death. Amen.

Prayer for a Happy Death

INFANT Jesus, full of mercy! I come to You. Bless
me in the hour of my death. When the hour of my
passing approaches, please, Infant of Prague, give
me an opportunity to have my last rites with the
Sacrament of the Anointing of the Sick, and with a
truly tender repentant heart be united with You in
the Blessed Sacrament. Stay with me, with Your
Holy Mother and Saint Joseph. Lessen my pain
and my fear; let me conquer all temptations val-
iantly; grant me the grace that I shall forsake my
earthly life willingly as compensation for my sins;
give me an assurance of eternal life.

O my dear Jesus, I pray You today already in the
name of Your pure Heart of the Holy Childhood,
deliver me from the lengthy pain and destitution of
purgatory and bring me to the enjoyment of everlasting happiness with You in heaven. Amen.

Prayer for Obtaining and Preserving Temporal Goods

O DIVINE Infant! source of all good, the goodness of Your Heart is infinite, and the bounty of Your little hand is immeasurable. Like a river, You pour forth Your gifts over thirsty mankind, and fill us with blessings in time and in eternity.

If You do not preserve our temporal goods, our industry will be useless and in vain. Almighty Infant, lift Your little hand and bless my temporal possessions; take them under Your powerful protection, and keep them from misfortune and loss. Give me the necessary grace to use my temporal goods according to Your will, to employ myself usefully after Your pleasure, and to give joy to my neighbor through love of You, that I may lay up treasure in heaven, where no thief can enter, nor moth nor dust destroy. Amen.

Prayer for Peace

D IVINE Infant, at Your entrance into the world You proclaimed peace, and You are pleased to be called the Prince of peace. You know the strife and discord in my house, among my relatives, especially N. N. You know how loveless and discontented we are with one another, how much strife, enmity, discord and hate rule in the midst of us, and how many sins we commit against the love of our neighbor.

This is a truly sad life! Where shall I turn if not to You, O peace-loving Infant Jesus! You have reunited those divided against one another, reconciled enemies, and given peace to troubled souls. Give us, I beseech You, the precious gift of peace. This I beg of You through the love and harmony You shared with Joseph and Mary.

Come to our aid, that all passions may be stilled, and that peace and harmony may return to me and N. N., that so we may deserve to be called children of God.

Prayer in Any Necessity

JUST Judge, You visit us men on account of our many sins, and threaten us with Your chastisements. We acknowledge that we all, one as well as the other, have deserved this punishment with which we are now afflicted. We humbly beseech You to pardon us, out of Your great-heartedness. Behold our good will, our contrite spirit, and our humbled hearts. We will never more offend You. Amen.

Prayer in Affliction

O DEAREST Jesus, tenderly loving us, Your greatest joy is to dwell among men and to bestow Your blessing upon us! Though I am not worthy that You should behold me with love, I feel myself drawn to You, O dear Infant Jesus, because You gladly pardon me and exercise Your almighty power over me.

So many who turned with confidence to You have received graces and had their petitions granted. Look upon me as I kneel in spirit before Your miraculous image on Your altar in Prague, and lay open my heart to You, with its prayers, petitions and hopes. Especially the affair of . . . I enclose in Your loving Heart. Govern me and do with me and mine according to Your holy will, for I know that in Your Divine wisdom and love You will ordain everything for the best. Almighty, gracious Infant Jesus, do not withdraw Your hand from us, but protect and bless us forever. Amen.

Thanksgiving for Graces Received from the Infant of Prague

O GENEROUS Infant Jesus, I prostrate myself before Your miraculous image and give my thanks to You for all the graces that I have received. I shall always praise Your infinite mercy and I confess that You are my God, my Helper and my Protector.

From here onward I shall place my trust in You and publicly proclaim Your Kingship and generosity; then everybody shall realize Your great love and the miracles that You have shown through this image. They shall honor and worship Your Infancy full of grace, in increasing numbers, and their hearts will remain in never-ending gratitude toward Your holy Infancy, which be hailed and praised in eternity. Amen.

Offering of One's Self to the Holy Child Jesus

ADORABLE Child, in whose bosom wisdom resides, Divinity dwells and all the eternal riches are enclosed. O beauty of heaven, O delight of the angels, O salvation of mankind. Source of innocence, of purity and of all holiness, here am I humbly prostrated at Your Divine feet, although a slave of sin, yet belonging to You by the undeniable right of Your sovereignty.

I hereby render to You as my Lord—my King and my dignified and most adorable Savior—my faith and my homage with the shepherds, my act of adoration with the Magi. I give myself entirely and without restriction into Your powerful hands, which drew all the universe from nothingness and preserve it in the admirable order that we see.

O lovable Child, grant that as a result of my total devotion to honoring the mystery of Your Divine Childhood, I may have the happiness through the mediation of Your Holy Mother and Saint Joseph, Your foster-father, to live all the rest of my life in the same manner as You. May I live in You, for You and under the direction of Your Divine Spirit, so that not one moment of my life deviates from Your will, or forestalls it in any respect, but listens to it and faithfully follows it in every way. Amen.

Remember, O Divine Child Je~

REMEMBER, O Divine Child Jesus, the promises You made to Venerable Father Cyril, Your pious servant, in favor of those honoring Your miraculous Image and the mysteries it reminds us of Your Childhood. Full of confidence in Your goodness, O Jesus, we come to submit our misery to You.

Grant us, by the infinite merits of Your Incarnation and of Your Holy Childhood, to triumph so well over our enemies and to remain so faithful to You, that we may deserve to be Your servants and to be numbered among Your friends on earth and among Your blissful in heaven. Do not reject our humble prayers, O sweet and almighty Jesus, but receive them favorably and be pleased to answer them. Amen.

Prayer to the Holy Child under His Title of Great Little One

O VERY amiable Child Jesus, known as the Great Little One, grant me the grace to understand all the deep truths expressed by this title and to realize its lessons. You are little by Your human nature, little by the state of childhood into which Your love has reduced You and by the rank You wanted to take among mankind, in order to enlighten and save us. You are a Holy Child.

But at the same time You are great, beyond any greatness. You are great by Your Divine nature, with the Father and the Holy Spirit, absolutely infinite. You are great by Your Person, the Person of the Word, in all equal to the Divine Persons of the Blessed Trinity. You are great by the splendor of mercy and the source of all our grace and holiness. This is why, Holy Child, You inspire us so much. To secure my salvation and to become worthy of it, I, too, must be little and great.

I am little by the imperfection of my nature, by the lamentable state in which original sin has left us, by the consequences of my own sins. But, in order to imitate Your littleness and humility, I must become aware of this state of mine; I must have a permanent conviction thereof, which will inspire my prayers and all my hopes in heaven, my attitude toward all my neighbors. I have to be little in order to resemble You.

I must also be great. This I am, by the eternal destiny You provided for me and all the possibilities of potential perfection You have created in me. I must become great by the reality of the virtues and of the grace, by the richness of the supernatural gifts, the aim of which is to make me similar to You, to take part in Your eternal inheritance, the heavenly beatitude.

Grant me, O Jesus, the grace to reproduce in myself the resemblance of Your Littleness and Greatness: Be, O Divine Great Little One, the model and the source of my salvation and my holiness. Amen.

Prayer of Teachers or Educators to the Holy Child, Protector of Children

O JESUS, Model of childhood, since Your earliest years, You visibly grew in wisdom and in grace before God and men. At the age of twelve, sitting in the temple amid the doctors, You attentively listened to them, You humbly interrogated them and forced their admiration by the prudence and the wisdom of Your speech. You so willingly received the children, blessed them and told Your disciples: "Let the children come to Me for theirs is the kingdom of heaven."

Inspire me, as You inspired the model and guide of the zealous teacher, St. Peter Canisius, with a deep respect and a holy affection for children, an inclination and a pronounced devotion to teach them Christian Doctrine, a special aptitude to have them understand its mysteries and love its beauties. Grant me, O Holy Child, to be zealous in my teaching apostolate by the intercession of the Blessed Virgin Mary. Amen.

Prayer of Parents to the Holy Child for Their Children

D IVINE Child Jesus, under the amiable and weak appearance of childhood, You are hiding the might and infinite wisdom of God. Please listen to our prayer and provide us according to Your love. It is You Who made fathers and mothers and

Who gave them, for their children, an ineffable participation in the love which You feel for Your creatures.

But, in contrast with Your infinite love, some parents' love is poor and limited; therefore, we have recourse to You, to obtain for our children what our affection desires for them and whatever else is much desired for them: the welfare of the body, the external welfare of the soul, what is necessary for their present life, and especially what will assure them the possession of eternal life.

Infant Jesus, You are the joy of Mary and of Joseph, delight of Your heavenly Father, salvation of the world and glory of the blessed. Let our children be our joy and Yours, in having them grow like You in age, sincere wisdom and grace before God and men, until the blissful day of their entry into heaven. Amen.

Prayer of Children to the Holy Child Jesus

BELOVED Jesus, Child of Nazareth, You were for children a model of filial love toward parents, of deference toward adults, and of obedience toward superiors. Help me always to look at Your example and endeavor to imitate these virtues and all those that have been Yours. In this way I will grow in age, in Your grace and in Your love. You live and reign forever and ever. Amen.

Consecration of Children to the Divine Child Jesus

O DIVINE Child Jesus, You love children who are well-behaved, pious, obedient, and diligent at work. I *(say your name),* in order to make myself more pleasing in Your eyes, offer myself and devote myself entirely to You, in the present as well as the future. I take the firm resolution to love You with all my heart and to endeavor to imitate Your virtues, especially humility and obedience.

Accept my offer and my resolution, O Jesus, my Divine Little Brother and my Savior, and grant me the grace to keep intact the innocence and the purity of body and soul and to grow always in piety, virtue and wisdom. Amen.

Greetings to the Child Jesus

HAIL, most loving little Jesus, sweetest love, far above all created love! I greet You, and in the desires of all Christendom I embrace You.

Hail, most charming little Jesus, noble Child of Nazareth, full rose of Jericho, blooming flower from heaven! Draw our hearts to Yourself and refresh them with Your sweetness.

Hail, most lovable little Jesus, living Bread of Bethlehem, innocent Lamb of Jerusalem, newly-born King of Judah! Receive us into the number of Your chosen servants.

Hail, most beautiful little Jesus, watchful Shepherd of the heavenly sheep, beloved fellow-Brother of all the children of men, delicate flower planted by the Holy Spirit in the virgin heart of Mary, bright daybreak rising out of the dark night to the joy of the whole earth! Drive away from us the darkness of sin.

Glory and praise be to You, tender, sweet little Jesus! From the depths of my heart I pray to and adore You because for the love of me and of all mankind You were willing to lie in the manger and to suffer such great poverty and misery. I thank and adore Your tender limbs and Your tender hands and feet, and I praise the inexpressible love which drew You forth from the bosom of the Heavenly Father, down to a poor and miserable stable.

Glory and praise be to You, noble little Jesus! I greet and praise You with the same fervent love with which Your Mother loved and praised You so intensely.

Glory and praise be to You, most beloved little Jesus, sweet delight of eternal blessedness. I greet and praise You with the same love which made You leave heaven and become a poor Child.

Glory and praise be to You, most precious little Jesus, joy and honor of Your Heavenly Father! I thank You through Your own sweet Heart which You have revealed to the whole world through Your birth. I greet You over and over again, most beautiful little Jesus, sweetest delight of the Father's Heart, refreshment of sick souls. I offer to

You my own heart for your eternal glory and service.

Jesus, crown, love, joy, bliss of virgins! Your love made You the Son of a virgin. May You be glorified and praised forever. Amen.

The Emergency Novena

(For the individual's urgent need)

There are different methods and forms of the novena in personal urgent need. However, disregarding this difference, it is understood that a prayer be said hourly nine times a day. (This should be, however, without tension.) The most popular from follows:

O JESUS, You said: "Ask and you shall receive, seek and you shall find, knock and it shall be opened to you." Through the intercession of Mary, Your most holy Mother, I knock, I seek and I ask that my prayer be granted.

(State your request)

O Jesus, You said: "All that you ask the Father in my Name He will grant you." Through the intercession of Mary, Your most holy Mother, I humbly and urgently ask Your Father in Your Name that my prayer be granted.

(Repeat your request)

O Jesus, You said: "Heaven and earth shall pass away, but My word shall not pass." Through the intercession of Mary, Your most holy Mother, I feel confident that my prayer will be granted.

(Repeat your request)

Personal Novena (Nine Day Prayers) to the Infant of Prague

(For the true understanding of the spiritual life)

FIRST DAY

VENERATE the holy head of the Divine Infant in order to receive the three Divine virtues: faith, hope and love.

Aspiration

What do I see? What bright gleam strikes my eyes? It is the beautiful crown that adorns Your head. Kings alone have crowns upon their heads. You too, O dearest Jesus, are a King, the gentlest, greatest and most powerful of them all. You are King since ever and ever. I prostrate myself before You and humbly praise Your most sacred head.

Prayer

Enrich within me the light of faith, I pray You. Strengthen my faith in Your miraculous Image, representing You, as the eternal King of heaven and earth, the Son of the heavenly Father and the Blessed Virgin Mary, who served You so passionately and nurtured You with loving care. O Infant of Prague, full of mercy, give me some hope, for I am afraid because of all my sins. Help me to love You in all and above all.

SECOND DAY

ONE worships the royal appearance of the Divine Infant in order to gain mercy for all sins.

Aspiration

Holy Child of Prague, I humbly kneel before You and look with awe at Your Royal Majesty. You like to change Your appearance according to the condition of soul of those who pray to You. Sometimes You look severe and scornful but soon You look sweet and friendly. When there are sinners before You, Your sweet face seems to be saddened. They may know You better after they have repented their sins truly. Do You wish perhaps to point to our instability in performing good deeds and to our fickleness?

Prayer

O dearest Infant Jesus! Remember that Your most gracious Image lay seven years in dust, forgotten in a dark room, and yet it did not lose its beauty. Cleanse the room of my soul from the dust and dirt of sin and bring back to it the original beauty that belonged to it at the time of Holy Baptism. Amen.

THIRD DAY

VENERATE the eyes of the Divine Infant to gain complete victory over temptations

Aspiration

Oh, You shine like the stars of heaven, most beautiful eyes of my most beloved Infant Jesus. I cannot look at You without feeling delight and happiness and ecstasy. How fortunate I am to have Your kind look! What pleasure to look at You. Your eyes reveal the sight not only of visible men alone, but mainly that of the invisible Deity. Your eyes bring delight and fear, love and respect to mankind.

Prayer

Truly, I resolved never to insult You again, my dearest Jesus. Yet, I am fully aware of my changeable mind and afraid that I could break my promise under duress of temptations. My evil desires, Satan and the world do not cease trying to make me fall. For they are my sworn enemies. Where shall I look for help and find it? Where else than with You, my Infant of Prague?

FOURTH DAY

ONE adores the mouth of the Divine Infant in order to gain the love of one's neighbor, including the love of an adversary.

Aspiration

What do I hear? What a miracle! You, a small Child, speak, speak through an image and ask men for compassion. You spoke clearly: "Have pity upon Me and I will have mercy upon you." As You once called to Your faithful servant Father Cyril, so are You still calling to us, sinners.

Prayer

How strongly You urge love of one's neighbor and one's enemies. You taught this by a marvelous example when You were on the cross.

Place a lock on my lips and a door before my mouth to keep me from offending my neighbor or sadden him by my tongue. Help me to live fully in accordance with the most important law of Christians, neighborly love.

FIFTH DAY

ADORE the hands of the Divine Infant to receive strength and patience in persecution, cross and suffering.

Aspiration

I adore Your holy hands; You were deprived of them for seven years. How cruel and full of mockery were those brutal soldiers who, as heretics, severed Your little hands from the Image. Is this the gratitude of Your creatures to whom You give so much of Your love? You Yourself asked, full of sadness and miraculously, to have Your broken hands replaced.

Prayer

Perhaps these broken hands of Your Image of Prague are a symbol of all Your sufferings that

You endured when still a Child: Your Circumcision and Your Flight to Egypt, and all the other ones in the mysteries of the Holy Childhood. I, although a sinner, do not want to suffer. Whenever there is offense or humiliation, pain or sickness, I like to complain and carry on and show my sadness. This must change; give me patience and joy to endure, because You love a joyful giver.

SIXTH DAY

FOR sincere humility one worships the Divine Heart.

Aspiration

Oh, how filled is this Divine Heart of the Holy Child of Prague with love for the poor children of men. It is aflame day and night and radiates rays of love by means of uncountable mercies that are bestowed on all men, even the worst sinners on this earth. This Divine Heart performs most gracious and loving acts, and most generous ones too, where It is worshiped as the Heart of the Infant Jesus of Prague.

Prayer

O great and most wonderful God in the shape of an Infant, how deeply ashamed am I. You are the Supreme Highness, holy and perfect throughout, and yet You are humble of heart; I, misery personified, a profound sinner, am arrogant and haughty. This is why I am without peace of mind. You could turn Your face away from me and justly so, because I am lacking virtues.

SEVENTH DAY

HONOR the breast of the Infant Jesus and you shall receive a blessed hour of death.

Aspiration

As the heretic soldiers ventured to throw Your Miraculous Image in dust and dirt hatefully and furiously, it was Your omnipotence, O most wondrous Infant Jesus, by which the breast of the Image remained unharmed, although made of wax. Who can believe that a statue made from wax, so fragile and tender, could remain undamaged? But this is the way it was.

What other meaning could this have but Your future exaltation? "The Lord upholds all that falls and raises up all those that are bowed down." This is the case with Your Image and with You Yourself.

Prayer

O merciful Infant Jesus! I come to You to pray for a happy and blessed hour of death. When my last hour approaches, please come to me. Also let Your Holy Mother and Saint Joseph stay with me. Lessen my pain and my fear, let me conquer all temptations successfully, and be merciful unto me that I may gladly give my earthly life in hopes for eternal life and reward, and absolve my sins.

EIGHTH DAY

A DORE devoutly the feet of the Infant Jesus, that you may receive merciful judgment.

Aspiration

Hail, O blessed feet of my Infant Jesus! During the lonesome long years You remained unharmed, You were forgotten. But now You are honored and praised to the great fear of Your enemies. Your holy feet walked many thousand steps to find the lost sheep and to bring them back. How many a hard and difficult step did You take for me during the thirty-three years of Your earthly life? I am grateful for every one of them now and forever. Grant that they were not walked in vain.

Prayer

O just Jesus, the Heavenly Father gave You the power and the judgment. Oh, that You could be my merciful, instead of severe, judge. Grant me the mercy to be reminded of the last judgment many times so that I may serve You truly and avoid Your condemnation. In the name of Your Holy Infancy, I pray: Do not be my judge; be my Savior.

NINTH DAY

W ORSHIP in the Name of the Divine Infant, in order to win deliverance from purgatory.

Aspiration

I look upon You as a small helpless child, forgetting Your Divinity. You are the true God, the same as the Father; the Blessed Virgin is Your true Mother, being so rightfully called the Mother of God. You are pleased when we honor Your Mother because You love her. Grant us the privilege of worshiping Your own Divine Heart. In the name of this, Your Immaculate and Most Beloved Heart, be merciful unto me.

Prayer

I am afraid that I will have to stay for a long time in purgatory, because I am lukewarm in my repentance and much too slow in gaining all graces. Once there, I will not be able to do anything on my behalf and will have to depend on the prayers of others. The dead are quickly forgotten.

Therefore, I beg of You today, my dearest Jesus, and in the name of Your purest Childhood, deliver me soon from the pain and loneliness of purgatory. Amen.

Prayer for a Particular State in Life

O LORD, I beg You to grant me Your Divine light, that I may know the designs of Your providence concerning me. Then, filled with a sincere desire for my soul's salvation, let me say, with the young man in the Gospel: What must I do to be

saved? All states of life are before me; but, still un-
decided what to do, I await your commands. I offer
myself to You without restriction, without reserve,
with a most perfect submission.

My lot is in Your hands. I make no exception, lest
perchance what I except be that which You will,
and because I am too short-sighted to discover in
the future the different obstacles I shall meet with,
if, without Your guidance, I lead myself and arbi-
trate my own conduct.

Speak, Lord, to my soul; speak to me as You
spoke to the youthful Samuel: *Speak, Lord; for
Your servant is listening.* I cast myself at Your feet,
and I am ready, if it be Your will, to sacrifice myself as a victim to You for the remainder of my
days, in such wise as You shall deem most worthy
of Your greatness.

Prayer for Religious Vocations

O LORD Jesus Christ, sublime model of all perfection, You are ever urging onward all privileged souls in their high aspiration toward the goal
of religious life. At the same time, You also
strengthen them so that they may be able to follow
You in such a noble way of life.

Grant then that many, recognizing Your sweet
inspirations, may have the will to correspond with
them by embracing the religious state and so enjoy
in it Your special care and tender love.

Grant in like manner that there may never be wanting those angels of Your charity who will represent You day and night at the cradle of the orphan, at the bedside of the suffering, by the side of the aged and the sick, who perhaps have no one on earth to whom they may look for sympathy and a helping hand.

Grant that humble schools, like lofty pulpits, may ever re-echo Your voice, teaching the way to heaven and the duties proper to each one's state in life.

May there flourish in every place gardens of chosen souls who by contemplation and penance make reparation for the sins of men and invoke Your mercy upon them.

Enlighten, O Lord Jesus, many generous souls with the fiery glow of the Holy Spirit, Who is substantial and eternal love. By the powerful intercession of Your most dear Mother Mary, stir up and preserve in them the fire of Your love, to the glory of the Father and the same Holy Spirit, Who together with You live and reign forever and ever. Amen.

Prayer for Priestly Vocations

LORD Jesus, High Priest and universal Shepherd, You have taught us to pray, saying: "Pray the Lord of the harvest to send forth laborers into His harvest." Therefore we beseech You graciously to hear our supplications and raise up many generous souls who, inspired by Your example and supported by Your grace, may conceive the ardent desire to enter the ranks of Your sacred ministers in order to continue the office of Your one true priesthood.

Grant that the continual promotion of religious instruction, true piety, purity of life and devotion to the highest ideals may prepare the groundwork for good vocations among youth. May the Christian family, as a nursery of pure and pious souls, become the unfailing source of good vocations, ever firmly convinced of the great honor that can redound to our Lord through some of its numerous offspring.

Come to the aid of Your Church, that always and in every place she may have at her disposal the means necessary for the reception, promotion, formation and mature development of all the good vocations that may arise.

For the full realization of all these things, O Jesus, Who are most zealous for the welfare and salvation of all, may Your graces continually descend from heaven to move many hearts by their irresistible force: first, the silent invitation; then generous cooperation; and finally perseverance in Your holy service.

Consecration to the Holy Child of Prague

O DIVINE Child Jesus, only-begotten Son of the Father, You are the true light that enlightens everyone coming into this world. It is through You that I am, it is through You that all things have been made, and without You nothing would be. It is therefore just that I devote mysef to You without reserve.

In gratitude for all the love with which You love me, I devote to You all the love my heart is capable of. I ardently desire to love You still more, to offer You a heart less unworthy of You. Accept this ardent desire, O amiable Child-God, and kindly bless it.

You have suffered for us and have borne Your infirmities, in order that we might one day deserve to be associated with Your eternal happiness. I want to unite my sufferings to Yours, so that You may give them merit and they may be sanctified. As You have been weeping for me, because of my sins, help me by Your grace to weep for them myself.

I also devote to You all my joys. I only have the ambition and the will to seek those pleasing to Your service, by the practice of the virtues taught in the mysteries of Your Divine Childhood. I beg You to help me by Your grace to acquire the gentleness, the humility, the childlike simplicity, the filial confidence and the perfect obedience, of which You gave me such a splendid example.

May I progress in holiness and one day possess the rewards promised in heaven to those who practice the lessons of Your Holy Childhood. Amen.

PRIVATE NOVENA IN HONOR OF THE INFANT JESUS OF PRAGUE

This private Novena may be made in your home or in church, before a statue or picture of the Infant of Prague, on any nine successive days, especially from the 17th to the 25th of any month, and in particular in December before the Feast of the Nativity of Christ the Infant.

O MIRACULOUS Infant Jesus, prostrate before Your sacred Image, we beseech You to cast a merciful look on our troubled hearts. Let Your tender heart so inclined to pity be softened by our prayers, and grant us that grace which we ardently implore.

Take from us all affliction and despair, all trials and misfortunes with which we are laden. For Your sacred infancy's sake hear our prayers and send us consolation and aid, that we may praise You, with the Father and the Holy Spirit, forever and ever. Amen.

ANOTHER PRIVATE NOVENA IN HONOR OF THE DIVINE INFANT JESUS

Meditation

DEVOTION to the Divine Infant encourages people to honor the infancy of Jesus. It is God's will that we honor all the mysteries of our Lord's life so that we may learn to imitate His virtues and make use of the graces which each mystery imparts for our sanctification.

Consequently devotion to the sacred infancy of Jesus is a source of great graces and blessings. It is certainly most pleasing to Jesus that we remember His infinite love in appearing among us in the form of a child to save our souls and to win our love and confidence. A child attracts love. It is easy to obtain everything from a child.

Our Lord Jesus Christ told us, "Unless you change and become like little children, you will not enter the Kingdom of God" (Mt 18:3). He not only taught us by word but gave His life as an example. He came among us as a helpless Infant to win our love. As a little Child, He was still our God and already by right the King of the Universe He had created and now had come to re-create.

Devotion to our Savior, the Divine Infant, honors the great mystery of His Incarnation. We acknowledge His Divinity and His Humanity, and rejoice in His great love that led Him to give His life for us.

The Word of God

"THE shepherds found Mary and Joseph, and the Baby lying in the manger; once they saw, they understood what had been told them concerning this Child."   —Luke 2:16-17

"A Child is born to us, a Son is given us; upon His shoulder dominion rests. They name Him Wonder-Counselor, God-Hero, Father-Forever, Prince of Peace."   —Isaiah 9:5

"God so loved the world that He gave His only Son, that whoever believes in Him may not die but may have eternal life. God did not send His Son into the world to condemn the world, but that the world might be saved through Him."

—John 3:16-17

Novena Prayers

Novena Prayer

CHILD Jesus, I have recourse to You by Your holy Mother. I implore You to assist me in this need, for I firmly believe Your Divinity can assist me. I confidently hope to obtain Your holy grace. I love You with my whole heart and my whole soul. I am heartily sorry for my sins and beg of You, good Jesus, to give me strength to overcome them.

I make the resolution of never again offending You, and I resolve to suffer everything rather than displease You. Henceforth I wish to serve You faithfully. For the love of You, Divine Child, I will love my neighbor as myself.

Jesus, most powerful Child, I implore You again to help me: *(Mention your request).*

Divine Child, great omnipotent God, I implore through Your most holy Mother's most powerful intercession, and through the boundless mercy of Your omnipotence as God, for a favorable answer to my prayer during this novena.

Grant me the grace of possessing You eternally with Mary and Joseph and of adoring You with Your holy Angels and Saints. Amen.

Prayer to the Miraculous Infant of Prague

DEAREST Jesus, Little Infant of Prague, how tenderly You love us! Your greatest joy is to dwell among us and to bestow Your blessing upon us. Though I am not worthy that You should help me, I feel drawn to You by love because You are kind and merciful and exercise Your almighty power over me.

So many who turned to You with confidence have received graces and had their petitions granted. Behold me as I come before You to lay open my heart to You with its prayers and hopes. I present to You especially this request, which I enclose in Your loving Heart: *(Mention your request).*

Rule over me, dear Infant Jesus, and do with me and mine according to Your holy Will, for I know that in Your Divine Wisdom and love You will arrange everything for the best. Do not withdraw Your hand from me, but protect and bless me forever.

I pray You, all-powerful and gracious Infant Jesus, for the sake of Your sacred infancy, in the name of Your blessed Mother Mary who cared for You with such tenderness, and by the greatest reverence with which Saint Joseph carried You in his arms, help me in my needs. Make me truly happy with You, dearest Infant, in time and in eternity, and I shall thank You forever with all my heart. Amen.

Note: One of the Litanies on pp. 47-59 may be said.

Prayer in Honor of the Divine Infancy

JESUS, Divine Infant, it is Your will that we honor all the mysteries of Your life so that we may learn to imitate Your virtues and make use of the graces which each mystery imparts for our sanctification. Accept the honor I wish to give You by my devotion to Your holy Infancy.

Jesus, You came to us as a child that You might win our love and confidence. I feel drawn to You as I would to a child, but a Child Who is also my God. I turn to You with the greatest confidence. You want to help me because You are goodness itself; You know how to help me because You know all things; You can help me because You are all-powerful.

The heart of a child is kind and generous. Your Sacred Heart, O Divine Infant, is infinitely kind and generous, because it is the Heart of my God and my dearest Friend. You loved me so much as to want to become human like me. You wanted to become an Infant not only that You might be an example to us, but also that You might be able to suffer for us, atone for our sins, and merit graces for our souls. I thank You for this.

Trusting in the infinite love and mercy of Your Sacred Heart, and relying on Your words: "Ask, and it shall be given you; seek, and you shall find; knock, and it shall be opened to you," I humbly place my request before You: *(Here mention your request.)*

Loving Infant Jesus, accept the honor I wish to show Your divine Infancy and have pity on me. I ask my favor in the name of Your Blessed Mother who so tenderly cared for You in Your childhood. I ask it in honor of St. Joseph who carried You in his arms and protected You.

But if You should not grant my request, I humbly resign myself to Your holy will, for You know what is best for me, and I know that You love as only a God can love. Give me instead the grace to know and love You more, to serve You better, and to save my soul. Amen.

Prayer to Center our Life on the Infant Jesus

O LORD Jesus, let me know myself, let me know You,
   and desire nothing but You alone.

Let me hate myself and love You,
   and do all things for the sake of You.

Let me humble myself and exalt You,
   and think of nothing but You alone.

Let me die to myself and live in You,
   and take whatever happens as coming from You.

Let me forsake myself and walk after You,
   and ever desire to follow You.

Let me flee from myself and turn to You,
   that thus I may merit to be defended by You.

Let me fear for myself, let me fear You,
   and be among those who are chosen by You.

Let me distrust myself and trust in You,
   and ever obey for love of You.

Let me cleave to nothing but only to You,
   and ever be poor for the sake of You.

Look upon me that I may love You.
Call me that I may see You and forever possess
   You. Amen.

Prayer

ALMIGHTY and Everlasting God, Lord of heaven and earth, You revealed Yourself to little ones. Grant, we beg of You, that we who venerate with due honor the sacred mysteries of Your Son, the Child Jesus, and imitate His example, may enter the Kingdom of Heaven which You promised to little children. Through the same Christ our Lord. Amen.